A Walrus' World

written and illustrated by Caroline Arnold

PICTURE WINDOW BOOKS
a capstone imprint

Special thanks to our advisers for their expertise:

Joel Garlich-Miller, Wildlife Biologist
U.S. Fish and Wildlife Service, Marine Mammals Management
Anchorage, Alaska

Terry Flaherty, Ph.D., Professor of English
Minnesota State University, Mankato

Editor: Jill Kalz
Designers: Abbey Fitzgerald and Lori Bye
Art Director: Nathan Gassman
Production Specialist: Jane Klenk
The illustrations in this book were created with cut paper.

Picture Window Books
151 Good Counsel Drive
P.O. Box 669
Mankato, MN 56001
877-845-8392
www.picturewindowbooks.com

Printed in the United States of America in
North Mankato, Minnesota.
092009   005618CGS10

 All books published by Picture Window Books
are manufactured with paper containing at least
10 percent post-consumer waste.

Library of Congress Cataloging-in-Publication Data
Arnold, Caroline.
A walrus' world / written and illustrated by Caroline Arnold.
p. cm. – (Caroline Arnold's animals)
Includes index.
ISBN 978-1-4048-5744-5 (library binding)
1. Walrus–Juvenile literature. I. Title.
QL737.P62A76 2010
599.79'9–dc22
2009033380

Walruses are divided into two main groups—Pacific and Atlantic. This book is about Pacific walruses.

Where they live: Arctic and subarctic

Habitat: shallow water by ice floes or land

Food: clams, snails, crabs, shrimp, worms; occasionally, seals

Length: males—10 to 12 feet (3 to 3.7 meters)

females—8 to 9 feet (2.4 to 2.7 m)

Weight: males—2,700 pounds (1,215 kilograms)

females—2,000 pounds (900 kg)

Animal class: mammal

Scientific name: *Odobenus rosmarus*

A baby walrus is called a calf. Dive into the ocean with a walrus calf and learn about a walrus' world.

It is spring in the Arctic. The frozen ocean is starting to melt. The walruses are on their way to their summer homes along the northern coast of Alaska. Paddling with wide flippers, they glide through the cold water.

A walrus herd can have from 10 to more than 1,000 walruses in it.

One walrus climbs onto an island of floating ice. Her long tusks help her hold on. She settles down to rest. Her baby will be born soon.

arctic tern

The walrus baby has just been born. His plump body is covered with short fur. The mother walrus holds her baby close with her flipper. She sniffs him and rubs his back with her whiskers.

The new baby is hungry. He snuggles up to his mother's belly and drinks her milk.

At birth, a walrus calf weighs 100 to 160 pounds (45 to 72 kg) and is about 4.5 feet (1.4 m) long. The calf is almost the size of a person.

The baby walrus is just a few days old, but it is time for his first swim. *Splash!* He tumbles into the water. *Splash!* His mother dives in, too.

The baby walrus swims for a short while. When he gets tired, he takes a ride on his mother's back. In a few days, they will join a group of other walrus mothers and their babies.

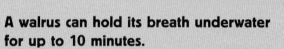

A walrus can hold its breath underwater for up to 10 minutes.

The baby walrus waits on the ice while his mother hunts for food. She dives to the ocean bottom. Using her whiskers, she feels a clam.

An adult walrus may eat up to 100 pounds (45 kg) of food a day. Young walruses begin to eat solid food when they are about a year old.

She squirts water from her mouth to loosen the clam from the sand. Then she grabs the shell with her lips and sucks out the meat. When she is done eating, she finds her baby and feeds him milk.

Now the ice has melted along the shoreline of the Arctic. All summer long, the walruses feed in the shallow water. Every few days, they come on shore. They crowd together in a giant noisy heap.

The mother walrus finds a quiet place at the edge of the group. She holds her baby close, and they take a nap.

In its first year, a walrus calf grows 4 to 5 inches (10 to 13 centimeters) a month.

As summer ends, the ocean begins to freeze. It is time for the walruses to swim south. The mothers and babies will join a male herd. They will all spend the winter at the edge of the ice.

For three long months, the sky is dark. When a cold wind blows, the walruses huddle together. Their thick fat keeps them warm.

The layer of fat under a walrus' skin is called blubber. It can be up to 5 inches (13 cm) thick.

In winter, male walruses sing long, loud songs to the females. They also fight on the ice. They raise their heads and roar. *Crash!* They hit one another with their long tusks.

16

The baby walrus' mother mates with one of the strongest males. In a few weeks, the male and female herds will separate. The young walruses will stay with their mothers.

Walrus skin can be up to 4 inches (10 cm) thick. Males have large, round bumps on the skin of their necks. The bumps are like armor.

The young walrus is now 1 year old. Inside his mouth, tiny tusks have begun to grow. He still drinks milk, but he is learning how to eat clams.

polar bear

One day, he spots a polar bear prowling on the ice. *Awk! Awk!* One of the walruses sounds an alarm, and the herd races into the water. For now, everyone is safe.

killer whales

The main predators of walruses are polar bears and killer whales.

The young walrus stays with his mother through the next summer, fall, and winter. The following spring, she gives birth to a new baby.

The young walrus is now 2 years old. He is ready to take care of himself. In a few years, he will join a male herd. The young walrus will keep growing until he is about 15 years old. By then, he will be an expert at life in the Arctic.

Where do walruses live?

Walruses live within and just outside of the Arctic Circle. Most Pacific walruses spend their summers in the Chukchi Sea, north of Siberia, or in the Beaufort Sea, along the north shore of Alaska. In winter, they live in the Bering Sea between Alaska and Siberia. Some travel, or migrate, up to 1,870 miles (3,000 kilometers) each year between their summer and winter homes. Atlantic walruses live in the waters of eastern Canada and Greenland.

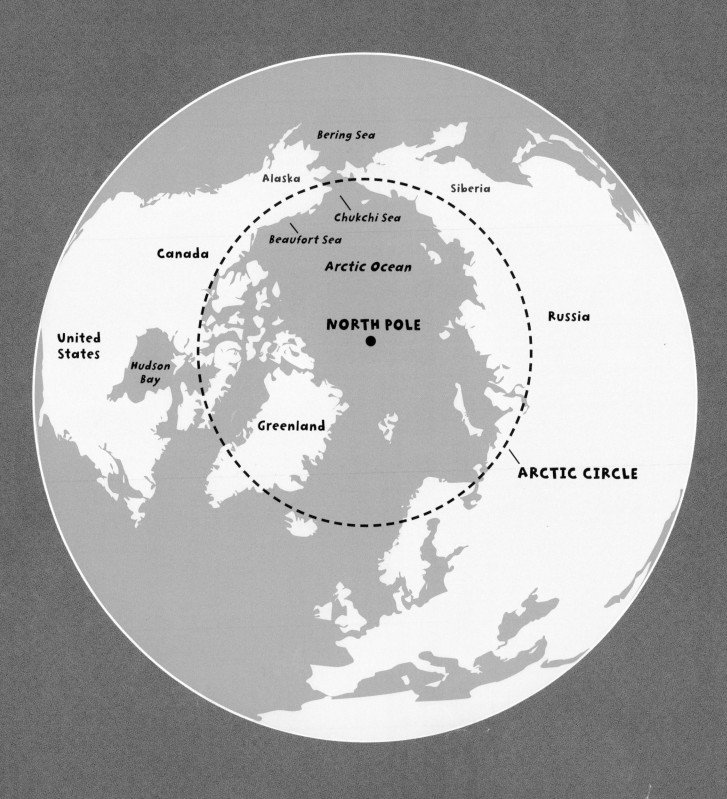

Walrus Fun Facts

Raising Babies

A female walrus has a calf about 15 months after mating. She cares for it for about two years.

Terrific Tusks

Walrus tusks are actually very large teeth. They are made of ivory. Females have tusks that can be more than 2 feet (60 cm) long. In males, tusks can be more than 3 feet (90 cm) long.

Tooth Walkers

Odobenus, the scientific name for a walrus, means "tooth walker." Walruses sometimes use their tusks like ice picks or canes for support on the ice.

Long Lives

A walrus can live as long as 40 years. Tusks grow a new outside layer each year. By counting these "growth rings" in a tusk, you can find out the age of a walrus.

Wonderful Whiskers

Both male and female walruses have 13 to 15 rows of stiff bristles, or whiskers, on their faces. The whiskers can grow to be 12 inches (30 cm) long.

Wing Feet

Walruses belong to a group of animals called pinnipeds, a scientific name meaning "wing foot." When swimming, they use their wide feet like wings to "fly" through the water.

Walrus Songs

Male walruses sing—even underwater! They whistle, beep, clatter, and make sounds like bells and harps. Their songs are so loud they can be heard 10 miles (16 km) away.

Glossary

Arctic—*the area between the Arctic Circle and the North Pole*

Arctic Circle—*the imaginary line parallel to the equator about 1,650 miles (2,640 km) from the North Pole*

flipper—*a broad, flat limb used for swimming*

habitat—*the place and natural conditions in which a plant or animal lives*

ice floe—*a sheet of floating ice*

mammal—*a warm-blooded animal that feeds its young milk*

mating—*joining together to produce young*

pinniped—*a kind of aquatic mammal whose four limbs are flippers; walruses, seals, and sea lions are examples of pinnipeds.*

predator—*an animal that hunts and eats other animals*

subarctic—*the area just south of the Arctic*

tusk—*a long curving tooth*

To Learn More

More Books to Read

Miller, Connie Colwell. *Walruses*. Mankato, Minn.: Capstone Press, 2006.
Murray, Julie. *Walruses*. Edina, Minn.: Abdo Pub., 2003.
Rotter, Charles. *Walruses*. Chanhassen, Minn.: Child's World, 2001.

Internet Sites

FactHound offers a safe, fun way to find Internet sites related to this book. All of the sites on FactHound have been researched by our staff.

Here's all you do:

Visit *www.facthound.com*

FactHound will fetch the best sites for you!

Index

photo by Arthur Arnold

Caroline Arnold is the author of more than 100 books for children. Her books have received awards from the American Library Association, P.E.N., the National Science Teachers Association, and the Washington Post/Children's Book Guild.

Caroline's interest in animals and the outdoors began when she was a child growing up in Minnesota. After majoring in art and literature at Grinnell College in Iowa, she received her M.A. in art from the University of Iowa.

Caroline lives in Los Angeles with her husband, Art, a neuroscientist. She has learned about wildlife of the far north at zoos, museums, and on a recent trip to Alaska.

Look for all of the books in Caroline Arnold's Animals series:

A Bald Eagle's World
A Kangaroo's World
A Killer Whale's World
A Koala's World
A Moose's World
A Panda's World

A Penguin's World
A Platypus' World
A Polar Bear's World
A Walrus' World
A Wombat's World
A Zebra's World

24